COBBLESTONE® · THE CIVIL WAR

Young Heroes
Of the North and South

Cobblestone Publishing
A Division of Carus Publishing
Peterborough, NH
www.cobblestonepub.com

Staff

Editorial Director: Lou Waryncia

Editor: Sarah Elder Hale

Book Design: David Nelson, www.dnelsondesign.com

Proofreaders: Meg Chorlian, Eileen Terrill

Text Credits

The content of this volume is derived from articles that first appeared in *COBBLESTONE* and *APPLESEEDS* magazines. Contributors: Roberta Baxter, Virginia Calkins, Suzanne Carpenter, James Collett, Julianne S. Condrey, Stephen Currie, Julie Doyle Durway, Meg Galante-DeAngelis, Sarah Elder Hale, Judith Lee Hallock, James Marten, Kathleen M. Muldoon, Patricia J. Murphy, Candice Ransom, Grace Bliss Smith, Stephanie Throne, Mike Weinstein, Sylvia Whitman

Picture Credits

Photos.com: 3, 4, 5 (top), 6 (bottom), 30, 32 (top), 40–41, 42, 43; Clipart.com: 6 (top), 25, 26, 27, 33; Beauvoir, The Jefferson Davis Home and Presidential Library, Biloxi, Mississippi: 7; Library of Congress: 5 (bottom), 8, 9, 10, 11, 14, 15, 16, 17, 29, 31, 34, 37 (bottom); Courtesy Massachusetts Commandery Military Order of the Loyal Legion and the U.S. Army Military History Institute: 12, 13; Fred Carlson: 18–19, 44–45; The Museum of the Confederacy, photograph by Katherine Wetzel: 20; Illustrations by Tim Foley: 22, 23, 24, 38; North Wind Picture Archive: 28; from Linus P. Brockett and Mary Vaughan, *Women's Work in the Civil War*, 1867: 32 (bottom); University of Connecticut, Storrs, Connecticut: 35; courtesy Mark H. Dunkelman: 36; courtesy of the Atlanta History Center: 37 (bottom). Images for "Civil War Time Line," pages 44–45, courtesy of Photos.com, Clipart.com, and Library of Congress.

Cover

Eastman Johnson, *The Wounded Drummer Boy*

From the Collections of the Union League Club, New York, NY. Reproduced with permission.

Library of Congress Cataloging-in-Publication Data

Young Heroes of the North and South / [project director, Lou Waryncia; editor, Sarah Elder Hale].

    p. cm. — (Cobblestone the Civil War)

    Includes index.

    ISBN 0-8126-7901-6 (hardcover)

    1. United States—History—Civil War, 1861-1865—Children—Juvenile—literature. 2. United States—History—Civil War, 1861-1865—Participation, Juvenile—Juvenile literature. 3. Children—United States—History—19th century—Juvenile literature. 4. Children—Confederate States of America —History—19th century—Juvenile literature. 5. United States—History—Civil War, 1861–1865—Biography—Juvenile literature.

I. Waryncia, Lou. II. Hale, Sarah Elder. III. Series.

    E540.C47Y68 2005

    973.7'083—dc22   2005015213

Printed in China

Cobblestone Publishing

30 Grove Street, Suite C

Peterborough, NH 03458

www.cobblestonepub.com

Table of Contents

Patriotic Children

A boy holding a Confederate flag called the "Stars and Bars" shows support for the Southern cause.

When we read about the Civil War, it is often stories about soldiers in battle or women on the home front. But adults were not the only people involved in the war. In every town and city, on every farm and in every school, children exercised their patriotic duty in their own ways. Whether Union or Confederate, children cheered their fathers and brothers in the army with letters from home. Children took care of the family homes and farms while soldiers were away in battle. And all children suffered from loneliness and the uncertainties of war, just as grownups did.

Raising Money

Children joined groups such as Soldiers' Aid Societies in both the North and the South. They organized fairs and raffles to raise money. Often they made and sold patriotic cockades — badges made of buttons and ribbon that celebrated the flag of the North, the South, or a state. Children performed in plays and concerts that had patriotic themes. Such entertainment often featured *tableaux vivants*, where costumed actors sat motionless and silent on a stage to re-create a famous picture or scene from history. Through these efforts, Northern children donated at least $100,000 to the care of the soldiers.

Care Packages

They also helped supply the soldiers with food and clothing. Children raised food that could be packaged and sent to the battlefront and made special treats of preserved fruits and jams for hospitalized soldiers. They made clothing, towels, and bandages that could be delivered to the field. Ten-year-old Emma Andrews from Ohio made 229 towels and handkerchiefs. The Canandaigua (New York) Young Ladies Society made 133 pairs of long underwear, 101 shirts, and many other clothing items in one year. Often, the children enclosed notes in the things they made to encourage and cheer the soldiers: "These stockings were knit by a little girl five years old, and she is going to knit some more, for mother said it will help some poor soldier."

When the war broke out, patriotic spirits were high. This illustration shows children raising the Union flag, with the nation's Capitol building in the distance.

Lula's Doll

A toy was part of one of the most famous events in the Civil War. Seven-year-old Lula McLean's rag doll sat in Lula's living room while Confederate general Robert E. Lee and Union general Ulysses S. Grant met in 1865 at Appomattox Court House, Virginia, to end the war. When Confederate general Robert E. Lee signed papers saying his army would fight no more, the war was over.

Making Do

Times were hard for people on both sides during the war. But life was especially difficult for children growing up in the Southern states. Union and Confederate soldiers marched through their towns and farms. The soldiers took food and livestock. They tore down fences and buildings for firewood. Schools and homes were turned into hospitals during and after battles. Everyday items such as paper and pencils were scarce. Like everyone else, children learned to "make do."

Twice-Turned Clothes

When kids outgrew their clothes, it was difficult to buy cloth to make new ones. Girls helped their mothers weave a plain cloth called homespun. When girls outgrew their dresses, mothers let down the hems. Shirts and pants were "twice-turned." That is, when they were worn out, they were turned inside out and then restitched to hide the worn spots. Old homespun clothes were unraveled and woven into new garments. Children dyed wool with colors made from onion skins, berries, and nuts. Boys and girls braided straw into hats and went barefoot to save shoe leather.

Young Hands at Work

With fathers serving in the army, children helped their mothers run their farms. Boys herded hogs, milked cows, and plowed. They planted wheat, and they boiled molasses. Girls made candles and soap with animal fat. They washed clothes in kettles of boiling water. Even the littlest children swept floors and dried dishes.

In 1863, young Anne Frobel of Virginia wrote in her diary: "...not an ear of corn, or grain of any kind on the place...." Boys planted crops, hunted, and fished. Girls picked berries and crab apples. Children planted and picked goober peas (we call them peanuts). Children learned to find food, too. Eight-year-old Sally Hawthorne of North Carolina gathered corn kernels left by the chickens. "We are so hungry," she wrote, "and it is so good."

Cornhusk Dolls and Whirligigs

As the war dragged on, everyone became tired of poor food and hard work. Children still found time to play, though. Outdoors, they played games such as fox-and-geese and blindman's bluff.

The Davis Children

Confederate president Jefferson Davis and his wife, Varina, lived at the Confederate White House in Richmond, Virginia. They had five children: Margaret (Maggie), Jefferson Jr., Joseph, William (Billy), and Varina Anne (Winnie). (Another son, Sam, had died earlier.)

The Davis children's nursery was filled with toys, books, pets, and a toy cannon. The nursery was next to their father's office and near the back stairs. This allowed the kids to see a lot of their dad. (President Davis loved this.) It also let them sneak in (and out) of the house in a flash.

The Lincoln Children

Abraham and Mary Todd Lincoln had three sons. Willie and Tad lived at the White House in Washington, D.C. with their parents. The eldest, Robert, was a student at Harvard University. (A fourth son, Edward, had died in 1850.) Willie and Tad got up to lots of mischief. Tad even built a fort on the roof of the White House. Their father loved to play games and hold contests with his sons.

Tad and Willie Lincoln, along with several other boys, formed a pretend band of soldiers. Once, the Lincoln boys' father — the president and commander in chief — "reviewed" the boy soldiers.

Boys carved animals and whittled moving toys like whirligigs. Girls made dolls from rags and cornhusks.

Children's magazines were filled with stories about heroism, bravery, selflessness, and patriotic duty. Everyone knew a soldier on a distant battlefield. And just like their fathers and older brothers, children answered their country's call. These patriotic children on the homefront did all they could for the soldiers of their army, North or South.

Drummer Boys and Fifers

Some of the North's and the South's very youngest took part in the Civil War. The Union army included several dozen boys who were not yet 11 years old, as well as hundreds of others who were under the age of 14.

The Confederates may have had even more youngsters. These youngest army members, however, rarely served as arms-bearing

Boys who wished to participate in the war often became drummers. This photo from 1863 shows the drum corps of the 93rd New York Infantry stationed in Bealeton, Virginia.

Key Players

Johnny Clem

The most famous Civil War drummer was Johnny Clem. Only 9 years old, Johnny ran away from home in May 1861 to enlist. An officer of the 22nd Michigan Regiment adopted him as a drummer boy, contributing the boy's unofficial soldier's pay of $13 a month.

Johnny saw action at the bloody Battle of Shiloh in April 1862. After a cannon shell smashed his drum, he became known as "Johnny Shiloh." Johnny later obtained a musket and fought bravely throughout the war. He became a sergeant after the Battle of Chickamauga in 1863. When he carried messages during the Atlanta Campaign, he was wounded twice and had one pony killed under him.

Johnny survived the war and chose to remain a soldier. He persuaded President Ulysses S. Grant to appoint him to the regular Army. In 1916, "Johnny Shiloh" retired as a major general.

soldiers. Instead, they were "armed" as musicians, bearing drums, fifes, and bugles.

Sneaking Off to Enlist

During the Civil War, boys were not supposed to enlist without their parents' permission if they were under a certain age, usually 18 years old. However, the rules frequently were bent. Boys who were turned down as soldiers often were accepted as drummers, fifers, or buglers. "The man behind the desk said I looked as if I could hold a drum," reported one such youngster, "and if I wanted I could join in that way."

There was never any shortage of boys anxious to "hold a drum." Most enlisted for what they saw as an adventure — army life seemed far more interesting than endless days in school or on a farm. Gustav Schurmann, tired of being a bootblack (boot polisher), spent most of the war drumming and bugling. He even became friends with President Abraham Lincoln's son Tad. Another drummer, Johnny Clem, was one of many who joined without his parents' consent. A few enlisted under assumed names, making it harder for their families to find them.

Learning on the Job

Although enlisted as musicians, most of the boys knew nothing about music.

"Went out to practice drumming," wrote C.W. Bardeen after joining. "Find it is no easy thing to learn to drum." Some, like Bardeen, switched instruments. And they learned soon enough, because once in camp, musicians had to summon the soldiers to meals and drills. That meant playing almost constantly. The resulting practice turned many boys into decent musicians.

Every part of the army's daily routine had its own musical call. The boys had to learn each one by heart. Musicians began the day with "Assembly of Buglers" and ended it hours later with "Extinguish Lights." In between came signals for soldiers to assemble for drill, to water their horses, and much more. The boys

Three drummer boys relax together in camp between battles and drills. Many of the young musicians had never played an instrument before joining the war and spent hours practicing.

This young freed slave found work as a drummer boy in the Union army.

usually grew weary of playing the same music again and again. The troops did not like it, either. As one soldier song complained, "I am sick of the fife, more sick of the drum."

Work and Play

Boys often took on other jobs in camp, too. Jerry Collins sorted mail. Bardeen built roads. Delavan Miller dug trenches. When given time off, the boys swam, sang, and played cards. Their drums even came in handy for fun. Boys sketched checkerboards on the drumheads or used them as writing tables. Also, most drums could be unscrewed from the top, so musicians could carry cards, extra food, or even a small dog inside.

Although boys could enjoy certain aspects of camp life, there was nothing fun about battle. Sometimes, buglers and drummers played amid the shooting, giving commands through their music. And musicians also worked with the medical corps. Otto Wolf helped perform amputations at the army hospital. "It is an awful sight," he wrote.

Under Fire!

Although musicians were unarmed, the fighting often found them anyway. "I was never so scared

Drumming Up Courage

Drummer boys sounded the daily calls and provided beats for marching drills. A well-trained regiment could maneuver expertly without spoken commands, with only the drumbeats transmitting the orders.

in all my life," Miller said about being pinned down by gunfire. Benjamin Fox was wounded at Kennesaw Mountain in Georgia. Charley King was killed at Antietam in Maryland. Some musicians showed particular courage during battle. J.B. Thomas grabbed a musket and fired into an oncoming enemy brigade.

Drummer boys, fifers, and buglers suffered from tragedy, hard work, and loneliness, just like their gun-toting brothers. They were far from family and friends. They struggled to do their jobs well. They saw men die on the battlefield. Yet many musicians considered their army years the best of their lives. (Because of their young ages, musicians in the Civil War were some of that war's last veterans.) As an old, retired U.S. Army man, Clem loved nothing more than talking with other Civil War veterans. Miller kept his drum, and 50 years later he described it as "loved and tenderly cared for." Harsh as the war could be for these youngest of soldiers, being a company musician was a source of pride for the many boys who took the job.

Key Players

Orion Howe

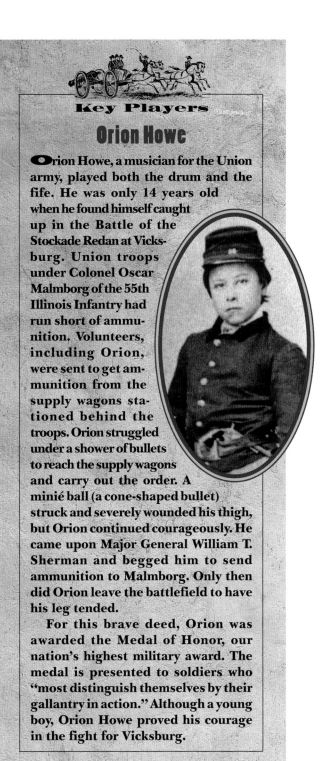

Orion Howe, a musician for the Union army, played both the drum and the fife. He was only 14 years old when he found himself caught up in the Battle of the Stockade Redan at Vicksburg. Union troops under Colonel Oscar Malmborg of the 55th Illinois Infantry had run short of ammunition. Volunteers, including Orion, were sent to get ammunition from the supply wagons stationed behind the troops. Orion struggled under a shower of bullets to reach the supply wagons and carry out the order. A minié ball (a cone-shaped bullet) struck and severely wounded his thigh, but Orion continued courageously. He came upon Major General William T. Sherman and begged him to send ammunition to Malmborg. Only then did Orion leave the battlefield to have his leg tended.

For this brave deed, Orion was awarded the Medal of Honor, our nation's highest military award. The medal is presented to soldiers who "most distinguish themselves by their gallantry in action." Although a young boy, Orion Howe proved his courage in the fight for Vicksburg.

Boy Soldiers of the Civil War

Many boys ran away from home and enlisted without their parents' permission. A worried mother or father would treasure a photo such as this one sent home by her son.

Although some of the youngest soldiers were musicians, a number of the older teenagers under the age of 18 actually fought on the front lines. Cadets from the Virginia Military Institute (VMI), for example, made up a significant part of the Southern forces at the 1864 Battle of New Market, Virginia.

Many of those soldiers were not yet 18, including North Carolinian William McDowell, who was one of about 10 VMI cadets killed in the action. "It was a sight to wring one's heart," an observer wrote. "That little boy was lying there [as if he were] asleep, more fit, indeed, for the cradle than the grave." Every May 15, VMI holds a special ceremony in memory of the cadets who fought at New Market. When the deceased's name is called during roll call, one of the present-day cadets answers, "Dead on the field of honor."

Several boy soldiers became famous for their courage. Michigan's Robert Hendershot crossed a river by clinging to the stern of a boat and captured a Confederate soldier on the other side. "Boy, I glory in your spunk," a Union general told him. Orion Howe of Illinois was shot at Vicksburg but refused to leave his post until he had delivered an important message about ammunition. Orion, only 14 years old at the time of the battle, was given the Medal of Honor.

Other boy soldiers were glad just to escape the war with their lives. Confederate John Delhaney spent nearly two years in a Union prison camp. Halfway through his first battle, Elisha Stockwell of Wisconsin regretted his haste to enlist. "As… the shells were flying over us," he remembered later, "I thought what a foolish boy I was to run away and get into such a mess as I was." Elisha survived the battle, though, and made it home after all. Famous or unknown, the lucky boys were the ones who managed to do the same.

The horrible reality of the war was captured in photos such as this one, showing a 14-year-old Confederate boy dead in a battle trench.

Fast Fact

More than
10,000
soldiers under the age of 18 served in the Union army.

Powder Monkeys

Young boys on Civil War ships had an important role. They were small enough to scurry easily down the hatch. They were fast enough and strong enough to run with a bag of gun powder. These boys were often dubbed "powder monkeys" by their grown-up mates. Besides keeping gunners supplied with gunpowder and ammunition, these boys had other jobs, too. They probably served in the mess, knotted and spliced ropes, sewed sails, and climbed to the tops of masts to spot oncoming ships.

Frederick Grant visited his father several times during the Civil War. He appears in this wartime photograph (seated to the left of Grant, who is standing, facing right).

'Three Cheers for Young Grant!'

General Ulysses S. Grant and his oldest son, Fred, watched from the gunboat *Henry Von Ahul* as the Union fleet steamed down the Mississippi River past Confederate batteries. Twelve-year-old Fred had begged to be allowed to accompany his father on the Vicksburg (Mississippi) Campaign. He was very excited.

Pitching In

Leaving Fred asleep on the boat, Grant went ashore the next morning to join his troops. When Fred woke up and realized his father was gone, he jumped ashore. Hoping to find the general, he joined a regiment marching to the front.

Instead, he found himself in the midst of the Battle of Port Gibson. When the fighting ended, Fred pitched in to help bury the dead and take the wounded to a house that was serving as a hospital. Exhausted, he finally fell asleep on the ground, where his amazed father later found him.

Mistaken Identity

Other battles soon followed. In the confusion after the Battle of Champion Hill, in Mississippi, a party of Union soldiers mistakenly tried to take Fred away as a prisoner. Luckily, an old soldier recognized the boy and yelled, "Three cheers for young Grant!" The red-faced soldiers released Fred and shouted heartily.

Once, as Fred watched retreating Confederates swim across the Big Black River, he was hit in the leg by an enemy sharpshooter. "I am killed," Fred told the Union officer who rushed to his aid. When instructed to wiggle his toes, the boy obeyed and realized that the wound, while painful, was not serious.

The Battle of Vicksburg

Vicksburg, Mississippi, was known as "the Gibraltar of the Confederacy," which meant that it was considered unconquerable. By the spring of 1863, it was one of the last Confederate-controlled cities along the Mississippi River. Both the North and the South recognized how valuable Vicksburg was. As President Abraham Lincoln said, "The war can never be brought to a close until that key [Vicksburg] is in our pocket."

Vicksburg surrendered to Union forces on July 4, 1863. Although the Civil War continued for another 21 months, most historians agree that this battle and siege on the western front played a crucial role in sealing the fate of the Confederacy.

Vicksburg Surrenders

During the siege of Vicksburg, Fred rested in his father's tent. There, on the evening of July 3, a messenger brought a note to Grant. Grant read it, then quietly told Fred, "Vicksburg has surrendered." A jubilant Fred rushed out to spread the good news to the troops.

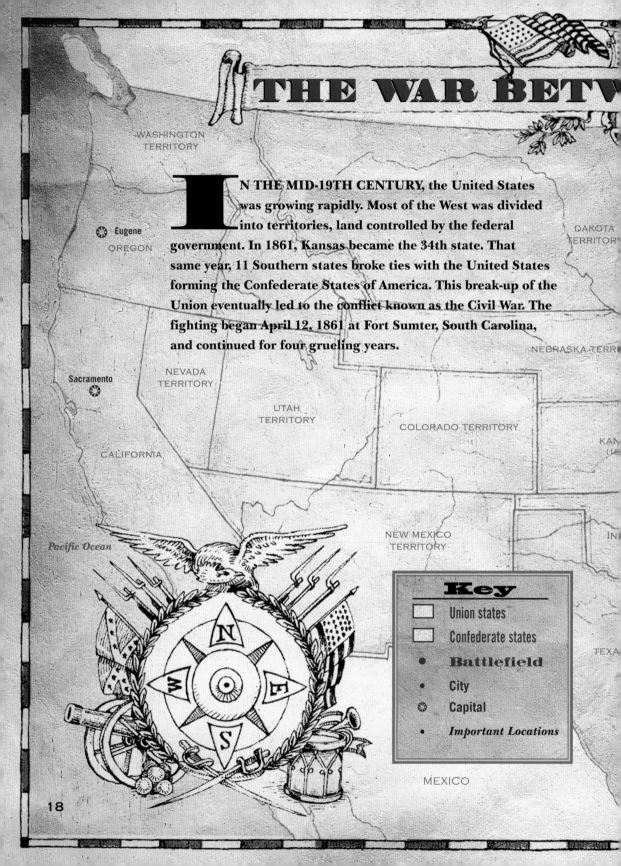

THE WAR BETW

WASHINGTON
TERRITORY

DAKOTA
TERRITORY

Eugene
OREGON

IN THE MID-19TH CENTURY, the United States was growing rapidly. Most of the West was divided into territories, land controlled by the federal government. In 1861, Kansas became the 34th state. That same year, 11 Southern states broke ties with the United States forming the Confederate States of America. This break-up of the Union eventually led to the conflict known as the Civil War. The fighting began April 12, 1861 at Fort Sumter, South Carolina, and continued for four grueling years.

NEBRASKA TERR

NEVADA
TERRITORY

Sacramento

UTAH
TERRITORY

COLORADO TERRITORY

KAN
(18

CALIFORNIA

NEW MEXICO
TERRITORY

IN

Pacific Ocean

Key

☐ Union states

☐ Confederate states

● **Battlefield**

• City

◉ Capital

• *Important Locations*

TEXA

MEXICO

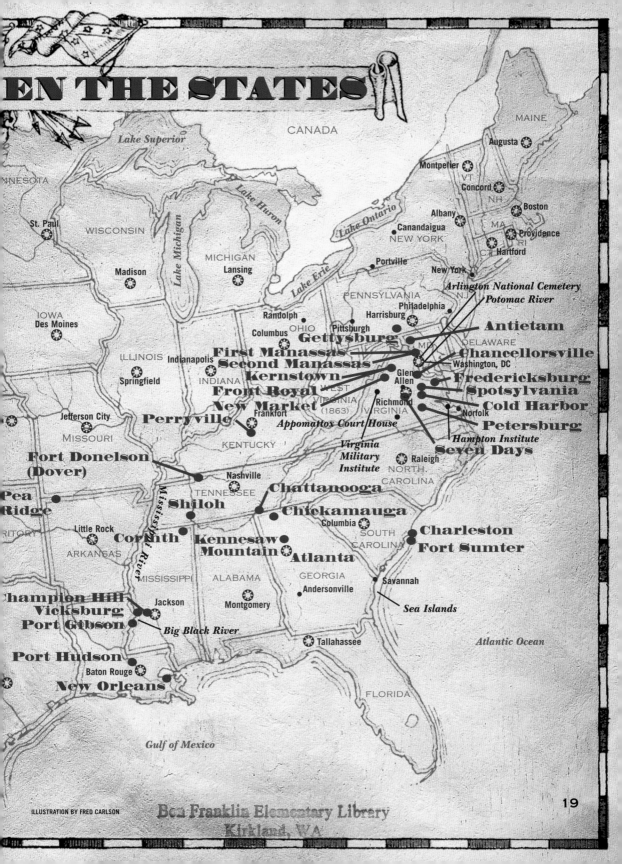

EN THE STATES

ILLUSTRATION BY FRED CARLSON

19

Caring for the Wounded

During the Civil War, attitudes about women began to change. Left on their own, mothers and daughters managed farms and businesses. Near battlefields, they opened their homes to wounded soldiers.

In the 1800s, most families cared for the ill at home. But war prompted the creation of more public hospitals. Nursing in hospitals was considered dirty work, suitable only for the lower classes, and preferably men. But the shortage of manpower during

The Civil War put women, young and old, in situations previously closed to them, such as nursing wounded soldiers on the battlefield and in hospitals.

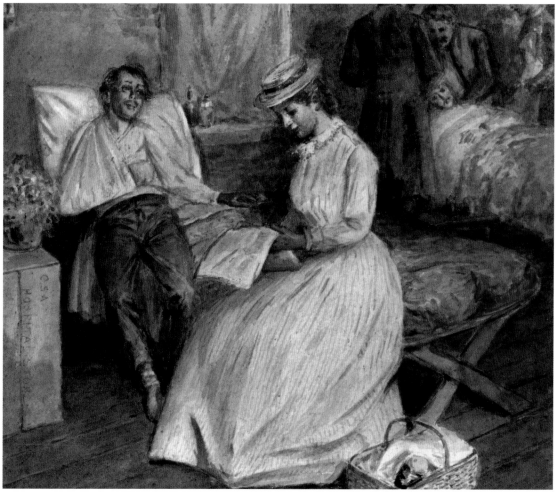

the Civil War drew women of all ages into new roles. The common notion that women were supposed to be delicate and quick to faint at the sight of blood began to fade.

Not much is known about the roughly 2,000 women who volunteered as Civil War nurses, most of whom worked in towns well behind the battle lines. A few kept diaries, but military records mention only names.

Captured!

In 1863, 12-year-old Delity Powell Kelly and her mother followed her father, a Confederate artilleryman, so they could tend to the ill and wounded. Delity must have served near the front — retreating troops did not have time to load the wounded into wagons and transport them to safety — because she was captured twice. The first time Delity was caught, in Florida, she and her mother escaped by breaking a window. The second time, in Georgia, the Confederates traded five Union soldiers to get Delity back. After the war, the Florida legislature voted her a Confederate veteran's pension for her bravery — the only one the state ever awarded a woman.

Emma Edmonds, a Union field nurse, described the horrors that Delity probably witnessed: "The sight of the [battle]field is perfectly appalling; men tossing their arms wildly calling for help; there they lie bleeding…. The ground is crimson with blood."

Little Training

Seventeen-year-old Jennie McCreary, a Union sympathizer, wrote about her experiences during the Battle of Gettysburg, Pennsylvania, in a letter to her sister. "I went over to Weaver's to help them roll bandages. We had not rolled many before we saw the street filled with wounded men…. I never thought I could do anything about a wounded man but I find I had a little more nerve than I thought I had."

Both Northern and Southern nurses worked during the war with little support or training. In the 1860s, medicine was a primitive science. But nurses did what they could to relieve suffering: sharing water from their canteens, changing bandages, and offering words of comfort.

Fast Fact

More than

2,000

women served as nurses during the Civil War.

Allen Jay, Conductor on the Underground Railroad

Folks in Randolph, Ohio, might not have noticed anything different about 11-year-old Allen Jay on July 1, 1842. He finished his chores, grabbed his fishing pole, and headed for his favorite fishing spot, just as on any other day. But within hours, he would become one of the youngest people ever to work on the Underground Railroad.

A Secret 'Train'

The Underground Railroad had no engine, train cars, or tracks. It was an enormous network of homeowners sympathetic to the plight of the slaves who secretly transported runaway slaves to freedom. In the years leading up to the Civil War, they hid the runaways and guided them from one safe place to another, but they had to stay one step ahead of the slave catchers who wanted to capture the slaves. Those who led the runaways to safe hiding places were called "conductors," the hiding places were "stations," and the escaped slaves "passengers." The ultimate destination for the travelers was either the Northern free states or Canada, where slavery was not tolerated and which slave catchers could not enter.

Allen's family belonged to a peaceful religious group called the Quakers, whose members were active in the Underground Railroad. Allen knew that African Americans were led to his parents' home in the middle of the night. He knew that his parents often fed and hid these runaway slaves. But he and his brother and sisters never asked questions. They understood that all visitors to their home were welcome.

On the Lookout

Allen had nearly reached the path leading to his fishing pond when a neighbor and fellow Quaker rode up to the Jay family barn. Allen stopped and listened. The man told his father that an escaped slave was hiding in the nearby woods. A team of armed men was after him. Jay sent Allen to the cornfield to watch for the man, lead him to the walnut tree in the center of the cornfield, and instruct him to stay there.

Soon Allen heard rustling in the woods. When he walked toward the sound, he saw a black man hiding in the brush. Allen trembled. He had been born with a hole in the roof of his mouth that made his speech difficult to understand. In slow, shaky words, Allen delivered his father's message.

Henry James

The man let Allen guide him to the walnut tree. He introduced himself as Henry James and begged Allen to bring him water. As Allen raced home, he wondered how he would get food and water for the man. His father had warned him not to say anything. But his

Fast Fact

By the time the Civil War broke out, Ohio had more than

229

antislavery societies.

mother met him with a basket of food and water and told Allen to "take it to whoever is hungry."

After Allen delivered the food and water, he returned home. A team of horsemen rode up to the Jay house. They asked his father if he had seen a runaway slave. Mr. Jay, who was bound by his religion to tell the truth, was able to honestly answer "no." But the men were not convinced. They vowed to return the next day with papers to search the house and property. (At that time, slaves were considered property, so slave owners had the right to search for and reclaim escaped slaves, even in free states.)

To Grandfather's House

That night, Mr. Jay asked Allen to drive to his grandfather's house. Henry James was hidden in the horse-drawn buggy. As they started out, Allen jumped at every sound and shadow. He expected men on horseback to overtake and shoot him. But James began telling him stories about slavery and how desperately he wanted to be free.

Soon Allen forgot his fear. They reached his grandfather's house safely, where an uncle waited with fresh horses to conduct James to the next station. Months later, Allen heard that James had arrived in Canada and was a free man.

Despite his speech disability, Allen became a minister, teacher, and well-known speaker. But he never forgot his first job as conductor on the Underground Railroad.

The Road to Freedom

The Civil War changed life for African American
children more than for any other American kids.
Before the Civil War, very young African Americans
lived much as other children did. They entertained themselves with
make-believe games. They played in the creeks. They adored their
parents. They had fun with other kids, no matter what those kids
looked like or how they dressed.

But African American parents must have felt great pain knowing

Slaves worked
long, hard hours on
Southern plantations
and farms, picking
cotton or harvesting
tobacco.

Fast Fact

A typical Southern plantation had

20

slaves.

Former slaves, freed by Lincoln's Emancipation Proclamation, were escorted by Union troops to contraband camps.

that their children were facing a life of slavery. Most African American kids were born into slavery because their parents were enslaved.

A Harsh World

As African American children reached eight or nine years old, the harsh world of grownups and slavery took over. A slave was under the control of another person. Slaves were human beings, but they were viewed as property, as a bicycle or a computer is today. It was illegal for slave children to go to school. Slaves could not leave their farms without the owners' permission. They had no freedom.

At one time, African American slaves lived all over the country. By the time of the Civil War, slavery had been abolished in the North. African Americans who were not enslaved, known as Free Negroes, were tolerated — but not always accepted — in the Northern states. A few African Americans in the South lived as Free Negroes, but most African Americans in the South were still slaves.

Following the Union

Many Union soldiers, who fought for the North in the Civil War, did not care deeply one way or the other about slavery. But their leader,

President Abraham Lincoln, freed the slaves who lived in the Confederate states when he issued the Emancipation Proclamation in 1862.

Whenever Northern soldiers marched into one of the Confederate states, slaves ran to them to freedom. Some African American parents rolled their few possessions in a blanket. Then they took their children by the hand and followed the Union soldiers. Considered *contraband* (smuggled

> ## Whenever Northern soldiers marched into one of the Confederate states, slaves ran to them to freedom.

property), they often lived in little towns called "contraband camps." These camps usually were found near where the Union army had set up its tents.

The former slaves lived in old packing crates, sod huts, and — if they were lucky — abandoned houses. One room might hold as many as six families. Children, like their parents, worked very hard. They planted and harvested crops, worked as servants to soldiers, or took care of younger brothers and sisters. It was a rough introduction to freedom.

Slaves lived together in simple houses. Even for children, free time was rare, and it was a luxury to relax.

Thirst for Knowledge

But most black children did manage to spend at least part of their time in school. Some worked in the morning and attended class in the afternoon. Young babysitters brought their infant and toddler siblings with them to school, letting them nap on the porch while

At schools for freed slaves, such as this one in Mississippi, children learned how to read and write alongside adults.

the older brothers and sisters studied inside.

Some schools were very small, like the one organized for several little black girls by the nine-year-old daughter of a Union army surgeon in Corinth, Mississippi. Others were quite large. For instance, 1,400 African American students attended public schools run by the Union army in New Orleans. And a woman named Lucy Chase opened a school in Richmond's (Virginia) First African Church that had more than 1,000 students!

Some teachers were African Americans, and some were former slaves. In 1861, Mary Smith Peake organized the first school opened by the American Missionary Association in Norfolk, Virginia. Peake was a black woman whose school eventually became Hampton Institute (now Hampton University). Many 19th-century and early-

Susie Baker King Taylor

Susie Baker was born into slavery on August 6, 1848. She lived on a plantation near Savannah, Georgia. When Susie was seven, she was allowed to live in Savannah with her grandmother. The move changed Susie's life. Although it was against the law for slaves to learn to read or write, Susie secretly attended a school run by a free black woman.

With the start of the Civil War, many African Americans began to hope that they finally might know liberty. For Susie, that day came in April 1862. The federal navy had taken control of the Sea Islands along the coast of Georgia. Her uncle fled to the protection of the Union fleet, taking his seven children and Susie with him.

Within a few days, Union military officials asked her to help educate other freed people. Susie soon taught 40 children and several adults, all of them eager to learn how to read and write.

At the end of 1862, freed slaves began enlisting in the 1st South Carolina Volunteer Infantry Regiment. Several of Susie's relatives joined, including her husband, Edward King. Susie became an army launderer, while continuing to teach the slaves-turned-soldiers.

In time, Susie added the nursing of the sick and wounded to her other army duties. She aided the surgeons and prepared special dishes for the suffering men. In June 1863, Clara Barton, who later founded the American Red Cross, met Susie while visiting several hospitals in the area.

When the war ended, Susie continued to educate freed people in the South. In September 1866, her husband died shortly before she gave birth to a son. Later, she moved to Boston, Massachusetts, where she married Russell L. Taylor. In 1886, Susie became active in the Women's Relief Corps, which aided veterans.

By 1869, approximately 150,000 former slaves were attending classes in about 3,000 new schools.

20th-century black leaders, such as Booker T. Washington, were educated there.

The subjects learned by these newly freed children were often the same as those studied by white children in the North: reading, writing, arithmetic, and geography. They used textbooks written just for them with names like *The Freedman's Spelling Book*.

Most former slave children were very serious about their studies, although sometimes they were mischievous. In one school, the students confused their teacher by trading names or making up new ones every week. One student even called himself Stonewall Jackson, after the famous Confederate general.

But education was clearly very important to the freed children who were lucky enough to attend school. This was proven to one Northern teacher when she asked a group of girls, "What good does it do you to come to school?" One of them replied, "If we are educated, they can't make slaves of us again."

Belle Boyd, Confederate Spy

A firm believer in the Confederate cause, Belle Boyd spied on Union officers staying at her father's hotel, and passed strategic information on to generals in the Confederate army.

When the Civil War began in 1861, Belle Boyd was only 17 years old, but she was a passionate believer in the Confederate cause. A beautiful Southern belle, she used her charm and flirtatious manner to secure information about Union battle plans and troop movements for the Confederate army.

Jackson's Valley Campaign

In 1862, Union forces occupied the town of Front Royal, Virginia. But the town's position, where the north and south branches of the Shenandoah River meet, made it vital to the defense of the Confederate capital, Richmond. In the spring of that year, Confederate general Stonewall Jackson led his troops on what became known as the Shenandoah Valley Campaign. By moving north, Jackson hoped to distract some of the Union troops from attacking Richmond. Jackson also fought for control of the Shenandoah Valley, which provided supplies to and

freedom of movement for the South. After losing to Union troops at Kernstown in March, Jackson went on to win all five battles he fought in May and June, which kept the South in the war.

'What's Happening?'

On May 23, 1862, Belle stopped on the street to speak to a Union officer with whom she had flirted in the past. Pointing to the wagons hurrying through town, she asked what was happening.

"Jackson is getting ready to attack. We're trying to round up our ammunition and supplies," he told her.

"What will you do with them?" asked Belle.

"Burn them," yelled the officer as he rode off. "And the bridges to Winchester, as well."

Spying From the Balcony

Belle had spied on a top-secret meeting of the Union generals the night before. The meeting had taken place in the dining room of a hotel owned by her family. She knew that Union troops under General Nathan P. Banks were gathering in a nearby town. Running up to the balcony of the hotel with a spyglass, Belle saw the advance guard of Jackson's forces, but they were moving slowly. Her knowledge of the Union plan would enable Jackson to attack first, before the Union troops in Front Royal could escape.

When Belle approached a

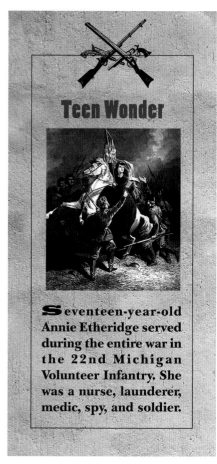

Teen Wonder

Seventeen-year-old Annie Etheridge served during the entire war in the 22nd Michigan Volunteer Infantry. She was a nurse, launderer, medic, spy, and soldier.

group of Southern loyalists, she begged for one of them to ride out to Jackson's camp with her information. When no one was willing to risk it, she was determined to go herself. Grabbing her white sunbonnet, Belle ran through back streets and jumped over fences and flower gardens. Gasping for breath, she reached the road that led out of town. Federal pickets spotted her and opened fire. A bullet pierced Belle's skirt. Moving quickly, she soon was out of range of the rifles.

Mission Accomplished

Suddenly, Belle noticed gray Confederate uniforms approaching. Staggering up the road, she was caught immediately in enemy crossfire. A minié ball whistled past her ear. To Belle's relief, Major Harry Douglas, Jackon's aide and an old friend of hers, rode up and recognized her. She gasped out her information to him and urged him to seize the bridges before the retreating Union troops could burn them.

Acting on her tip, General Richard Taylor signaled the bugler to sound the charge. Waves of troops raced down the hill. Jackson appeared at the top, surprised to find the attack had begun. Union soldiers fled over the bridges and set them ablaze, but the Confederates managed to put out the fires and pursue the Union soldiers north. Belle's information allowed Jackson's forces to capture the Front Royal garrison and valuable enemy supplies. Jackson was introduced to Belle that day and later wrote her a personal note of thanks. He made her an honorary member of his staff, with the rank of captain.

Betrayed!

Union forces recaptured Front Royal a week later. In July, Belle was denounced as a spy. Some historians say she was betrayed by a female prisoner from the North who had been entrusted to her care; others say she was betrayed by her sweetheart. Belle was arrested and imprisoned in Washington for a month. She was arrested again in 1863 and released six months later. Belle Boyd always believed that one person could make a difference. She continued to spy for the Confederate cause and never wavered in her dedication.

A group of young boys huddle at the base of a church pillar in Charleston, South Carolina, after a battle in February 1865 left parts of the city in ruins.

Orphans of the War

On Thanksgiving Day 1863, two little children knocked on the door of the governor's mansion in Harrisburg, Pennsylvania. They said that their father had died fighting with the Union army. Andrew Curtin, Pennsylvania's governor, was very moved after meeting them. He decided the state should take care of the hundreds of boys and girls left without fathers after the war. The Pennsylvania Railroad donated $50,000, and eventually 15 "orphan schools" were set up for Pennsylvania's war orphans.

On Their Own

Even before the Civil War ended, Americans began to realize that something had to be done for the many children of killed and crippled soldiers. Places like the New York Newsboys' Lodging House in New York City and the Northern Home for Friendless Children in Philadelphia, Pennsylvania, already were taking in large numbers of fatherless children. Religious groups across the country also responded to the need.

Orphanages were built throughout the eastern states for homeless children. This one in Storrs, Connecticut, later became an agricultural school. It is now part of the University of Connecticut.

Several schools and homes were created especially for African American children. Having run away from their Southern owners or having parents who died, these children were homeless and on their own.

Many of the children accepted into various institutions were not really orphans, however. In some cases, their fathers had died while serving in the army, and their mothers were too poor or sick to take care of them. Some had no mothers, and their fathers were in the army. Or, after the war, some children were left with one parent who had to work long hours in a factory or on a farm. Some men had no choice but to give up their sons and daughters to orphanages because they could not take care of them alone. Children with only one parent often were called "half orphans."

Orphan Homes

Most Northern states built special places for soldiers' orphans. These were paid for with tax money. Although they started small, some grew into large institutions that began accepting all orphans, not just those who were casualties of war. Other homes were supported by groups of Union veterans such as the Grand Army of the Republic. In Indiana, for instance, orphaned children lived in the same dwelling as crippled soldiers. In 1870, when the number of children grew larger than the number of soldiers, a separate residence was built.

The most famous orphan home grew out of a national search for the children of a dead soldier. Found killed on the battlefield at Gettysburg, Pennsylvania, in 1863, he clutched in his hand a picture of two young boys and a young girl. No one knew who this soldier-father was, but newspapers and magazines all over the country ran the picture. It created a wave of sympathy for the nameless children. A song was written based on the story. Called "The Children of the Battlefield," it was published as sheet music, with the picture of the children on the front cover.

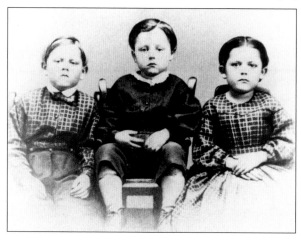

This photo was found in the hand of a dead soldier at Gettysburg, later identified as Sergeant Amos Humiston. An outpouring of sympathy for the children — Frank, Alice, and Fred — led to the establishment of an orphanage in Gettysburg.

Eventually the family of the dead soldier — Sergeant Amos Humiston — was found in Portville, New York. His widow, Philinda, received some of the money from the sale of the picture and the music. But much of the money was used to establish the National Homestead in Gettysburg, which became a home for the children of dead Union soldiers. Mrs. Humiston was hired as its first matron, or administrator. By the early 1870s, 70 children were living at the National Homestead.

Laying Flowers, Waving Flags

The children who lived in homes for soldiers' orphans often took part in celebrations on holidays like Memorial Day and Independence Day. On Decoration Day (which later became Memorial Day), children at the National Homestead laid flowers on the graves of the Union soldiers who had been killed at Gettysburg.

Soldiers' orphans in New Jersey "brought tears to eyes unused to weep," said one adult spectator, when they sang patriotic songs at a flag raising on Independence Day. Drill teams and bands from orphan homes also took part in veterans' reunions and helped dedicate monuments to Civil War heroes.

Two Girls, Two Diaries

Caroline Richards and Carrie Berry were real girls who grew up in the 1860s. Each kept a diary during the Civil War.

Girls growing up at the time of the Civil War had different experiences depending upon where they lived. Most Northern girls lived far away from the actual battlegrounds of the war. For Southern girls, the war was often fought in their own backyards.

Patriotism and Support
Caroline Richards, New York

Caroline Richards lived with her grandparents and younger sister, Anna, in a small town in New York. For the most part, her daily life during the war was unchanged. She still went to school and church, attended concerts, and helped with household chores. News of the war came through reading newspapers and listening to stories told by friends and relatives.

In her diary, Caroline wrote about the importance of showing support for the Union soldiers. "A lot of us girls went down to the train and took flowers to the soldiers as they were passing through," she wrote in May 1861. "We wear little flag pins for badges and tie our hair with red, white, and blue ribbon."

Caroline also helped sew garments and bandages for the soldiers: "We are going to write notes and enclose them in the garments to cheer up the soldier boys." When the war ended in 1865, she joined in the celebration: "I am going down town…with my flag in one hand and bell in the other and make all the noise I can." For Caroline Richards, the Civil War was a time to show patriotism for her country.

Hardship and Fear
Carrie Berry, Georgia

Growing up in Atlanta, Georgia, Carrie Berry had very different wartime experiences. With her parents and sister, Carrie lived

Hams in Hiding

Personal stories of the Civil War have survived in journals, letters, and family histories. This fictional account is based on a story passed down by the Sheppard family of Glen Allen, Virginia. It tells of a time in May 1864 when Union troops under General Philip Sheridan were passing through Glen Allen on their way to meet Confederate general J.E.B. Stuart's cavalry near Richmond, Virginia.

It sounded like the biggest thunderstorm Mike Sheppard had heard during his 13 years in Virginia. Looking up, he could not see any storm clouds that might be causing such a roar. Something just did not seem right. Mike stopped his work and unhitched the two horses that had not been seized by the Confederate army. Hopping onto one of them, he rode down the path through the apple orchard.

When Mike reached the road, he jumped down off the horse and saw row after row of Union cavalrymen riding east down the road. It seemed to be a never-ending sea of blue.

Mike jumped as a twig snapped nearby. "Psst," someone said. It was Lizzie, his 11-year-old sister, who was hiding in the bushes. Her eyes were wide as she watched the soldiers. "I was picking wild strawberries and I came to see what all the noise was…." Without waiting to hear more, Mike grabbed Lizzie by the arm and pulled her back into the woods.

Mike and Lizzie were well aware of the possibility of raiders finding their way to the Sheppard home. With his father away, Mike felt it was his responsibility to protect his mother and seven sisters. He had to act fast. "Lizzie, go tell Mother what we've seen. I need to tend to something," Mike said. As Lizzie ran home to warn her mother, Mike ran in the opposite direction to the smokehouse.

Leaping toward the meat hanging from the beams in the smokehouse, Mike pulled them off the hooks. He quickly wrapped up the hams in some worn fabric. With his heart beating fast, Mike grabbed bunches of herbs that had been hung up to dry. He ran to the side entrance of the house and into his parents' room. Throwing open their wardrobe, Mike made his way behind all the clothing and placed the hams along the back wall. He set the herbs in front of the hams, let the clothing fall back

into place, and quickly shut the doors.

Mike then found his squirrel gun. It was not much of a weapon against soldiers, he thought, but at least it was something. He sat and watched from the front porch of the house with his gun in his lap. He felt his hands perspire and a lump form in his throat as he saw blue-uniformed soldiers approaching on horseback.

The soldiers carelessly tramped through Mrs. Sheppard's flowerbeds. Two of the men rode off toward the vegetable garden to see what they could find, while another three rode up toward the house. Mike no longer knew if it was thunder, horses' hooves, marching soldiers, or his own heartbeat that was hammering in his ears.

As the soldiers approached the house and saw Mike guarding it, they saluted. Mike watched the hungry soldiers scour the house, searching for food. The soldiers rode off, carrying the few early vegetables the garden had produced. They also took the remaining coffee and fresh biscuits from Lizzie's birthday celebration two days earlier. They left behind the unripe sweet potatoes and herbs, as well as the precious hams in hiding.

through the shelling and burning of Atlanta by General William Tecumseh Sherman's Union troops in 1864.

For Carrie, each day brought new hardships and fears. On her birthday, she did not have a cake because of food shortages, so she "celebrated with ironing." Two days later, she wrote: "I knit all morning. In the evening, we had to run to Auntie's and get in the cellar. We did not feel safe in our cellar, they [the shells] fell so thick and fast!" (The Berry family had dug a hole in the ground where they hid when the fire from guns and cannon was heavy.)

As the fighting around Atlanta continued, Carrie could not go to school or anywhere else. She wrote: "There is a fire in town nearly every day. I get so tired of being housed up all the time. The shells get worse and worse every day. O that something would stop them."

When the Confederate troops abandoned Atlanta in September 1864, Sherman ordered everyone to leave the city, and then he set fire to it. By agreeing to work for the Union army, Carrie's father made it possible for his family to stay in Atlanta. But Carrie was not spared from the terror of a city being burned all around her.

"I could not go to sleep for fear that they would set our house on fire," Carrie wrote on November 12, 1864. When the Union troops finally left, Carrie wrote that she was glad, because "nobody knows what we have suffered since they came in." Unlike Caroline Richards, Carrie Berry was not sheltered from the brutalities of the war.

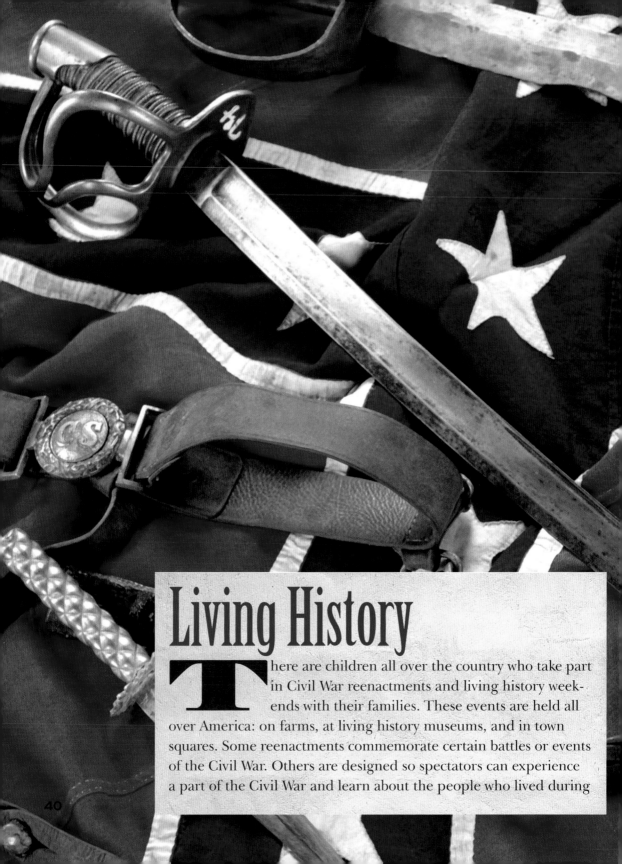

Living History

There are children all over the country who take part in Civil War reenactments and living history weekends with their families. These events are held all over America: on farms, at living history museums, and in town squares. Some reenactments commemorate certain battles or events of the Civil War. Others are designed so spectators can experience a part of the Civil War and learn about the people who lived during

Reenactors and collectors of Civil War artifacts are avid historians. These Confederate items have been carefully preserved so that future generations can feel connected to the distant past.

A family photo was often a soldier's most treasured belonging. Left: The three stripes on this Confederate uniform indicate it belonged to a sergeant.

the 1860s. Such events may involve just a few people, or as many as several thousand people.

True to History

Known as *reenactors*, these children (and adults) do their best to be true to all aspects of Civil War times. Reenactors try to look and act exactly as people would have in the 1860s. All their clothing must be of Civil War–period style and made of all-natural fabrics. Everything they use must have been available in the 1860s. At reenactments, *sutlers* sell clothes and equipment appropriate to the period.

At these events, reenactors do particular impressions, pretending to be certain kinds of people. There are two kinds of impressions: military and civilian. A few children are musicians trained to play the military tunes of the time. Almost all children do civilian impressions — they represent the life of the average child who lived during the 1860s.

Battles, Chores, and Games

Civilian children have much to do at reenactments. There are battles to watch, sutler stores at which to shop, and even school to attend. Civil War families set up their canvas tents in a civilian camp, away from the military camp.

In a civilian camp, children reenact 1860s chores. They gather wood and help cook the family meals over an open fire. Sometimes, they pick fruit from nearby orchards or berries from the woods for special treats. Children fetch water for drinking and washing. They help clean up after meals and even wash their clothes by hand!

One of the best things about reenacting is playing the many games from the time period. Games using imagination — such as charades, guessing games, and riddles — were very popular. Contests and races of all kinds also were enjoyed, as children spent a lot of time

outdoors playing with what nature provided. Music, too, was very important to children. Many played instruments and sang for enjoyment.

The Civil War was not just about battles. Children who reenact give others a broader view of the history of the 1860s. When spectators see children at a reenactment holding a fair to raise money for invalid soldiers or sewing handkerchiefs for a father who is away at battle, they are learning through living history. These young teachers and historians give us a glimpse of what it was like to live during the Civil War years.

This uniform belonged to Pierre Beauregard, the Confederate general who led the attack on Fort Sumter. Left: Soldiers passed the time in camp with games of checkers, cards, and dice.

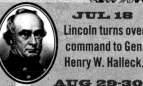

1860

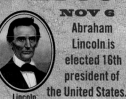

Lincoln

NOV 6
Abraham Lincoln is elected 16th president of the United States.

1861

Davis

FEB 9
Formation of the Confederate States of America (CSA) by secessionist states South Carolina, Mississippi, Florida, Alabama, Georgia, Louisiana, and Texas. Jefferson Davis elected CSA president.

MAR 4
Lincoln's inauguration

APR 12

Fort Sumter (South Carolina) Civil War begins with Confederate attack under Gen. Pierre Beauregard.

APR 15
Lincoln issues proclamation calling

for 75,000 troops. Gen. Winfield Scott becomes commander of Union army.

APR 17
Virginia joins CSA, followed by Arkansas, Tennessee, and North Carolina.

APR 20
Gen. Robert E. Lee resigns from U.S. Army and accepts command in Confederate army.

JUL 21
First Manassas (Virginia) Gen. Thomas J. "Stonewall" Jackson defeats Gen. Irvin McDowell.

NOV 1
Gen. George B. McClellan assumes command of Union forces.

1862

FEB 11-16
Fort Donelson (Tennessee) Gen. Ulysses S. Grant breaks major Confederate stronghold.

MAR
McClellan begins Peninsular Campaign, heading to Richmond,

Virginia, the Confederate capital.

APR 6-7
Shiloh (Tennessee) Grant defeats Beauregard and Gen. A.S. Johnston. Heavy losses on both sides.

APR 24

New Orleans (Louisiana) Gen. David Farragut leads 17 Union gunboats up Mississippi River and takes New Orleans, the South's most important seaport.

JUN 25-JUL 1
Seven Days (Virginia) Six major battles are fought over seven days near Richmond, Virginia. Lee is victorious, protecting the Confederate capital from Union occupation.

Halleck

JUL 18
Lincoln turns over command to Gen. Henry W. Halleck.

AUG 29-30
Second Manassas (Virginia) Jackson and Gen. James Longstreet defeat Gen. John Pope.

SEP 17
Antietam (Maryland) McClellan narrowly defeats Lee. Bloodiest day in American military history: 23,000 casualties.

SEP 22

Lincoln issues preliminary Emancipation Proclamation, freeing slaves in Confederate states.

OCT 3-4
Corinth (Mississippi) Gen. William Rosecrans defeats Gen. Earl Van Dorn.

NOTE: Battles are in black type, with flags indicating: Union victory ▀ Confederate victory ⊠

TIME LINE

NOV 7
Lincoln replaces McClellan with Gen. Ambrose Burnside to lead Army of the Potomac.

Burnside

DEC 13
Fredericksburg
(Virginia)
Lee defeats Burnside.

1863

JAN 1
Final Emancipation Proclamation frees slaves in Confederate states. Union army begins enlisting black soldiers.

JAN 25
Lincoln replaces Burnside with Gen. Joseph Hooker.

Hooker

JAN 29
Grant is placed in command of the Union army in the West.

MAY 1-4
Chancellorsville
(Virginia)
Lee defeats Hooker.

JUN 28
Lincoln replaces Hooker with Gen. George E. Meade.

JUL 1-3

Gettysburg
(Pennsylvania)
Meade defeats Lee.

JUL 4
Vicksburg
(Mississippi)
After weeks of seige, Grant takes the Confederate stronghold on Mississippi River, effectively dividing eastern and western Confederate forces.

SEP 18-20
Chickamauga
(Georgia)
Gen. Braxton Bragg defeats Rosecrans.

OCT 16
Lincoln puts Grant in charge of all western operations.

NOV 19
Lincoln delivers the Gettysburg Address, dedicating the

battlefield as a national cemetery.

NOV 23-25
Chattanooga
(Tennessee)
Grant defeats Bragg.

1864

MAR 9
Lincoln puts Grant in command of entire Union army. Gen. William T. Sherman takes over western operations.

MAY 8-21
Spotsylvania
(Virginia)
Grant defeats Lee.

MAY 31- JUN 12
Cold Harbor
(Virginia)
Lee defeats Grant and Meade.

JUN 15-18

Petersburg
(Virginia)
Lee and Beauregard defeat Grant and Meade.

NOV 8
Lincoln is re-elected.

NOV 15- DEC 21

Sherman's "March to the Sea." Sherman destroys supplies and transportation systems from Atlanta to Savannah (Georgia), crippling the Confederacy.

Lee

1865

APR 2
Petersburg
(Virginia)
Grant defeats Lee. Confederates leave Richmond.

APR 9
Lee surrenders to Grant at Appomattox Court House, Virginia.

APR 14
Lincoln is shot by John Wilkes Booth at Ford's Theatre, Washington, D.C. He dies the following morning.

DEC 6
Thirteenth Amendment to the Constitution abolishing slavery is ratified.

GRAPHICS BY FRED CARLSON

45

Glossary

Abolish: To get rid of completely.

Ammunition: Anything that can be thrown or shot — such as a bullet, rock, or cannonball — for use in attack or defense.

Artilleryman: A soldier who, as part of a team, mans heavy weaponry, such as cannon.

Belle: A popular, attractive girl or young lady.

Bondage: Bound to serve another with practically no hope of freedom.

Cadet: A student at a military school who is training to be an officer.

Campaign: In military terms, a series of battles, or other operations, in a particular area to accomplish a specific goal.

Casualties: In war, the victims: the injured, killed, captured, or missing in action.

Cavalryman: A soldier who is trained to fight on horseback.

Civilian: A person who is not an active member of the military or police.

Commemorate: To observe or honor the memory of a person or event.

Confederacy: In the American Civil War, the alliance of states that broke ties with the U.S. government to form a new government, called the Confederate States of America. The states

that did not secede supported the Union.

Contraband: Smuggled goods. During the Civil War, it was a term used to describe an escaped slave behind Union lines.

Enlist: Sign up for service in the military.

Garrison: A military post.

Hatch: An opening, especially in a ship or aircraft, to pass between sections or into compartments.

Infantry: The branch of the military consisting of soldiers who are trained to fight on foot.

Legislature: A group of elected representatives whose job it is to make laws that govern a state or nation.

Minié ball: A cone-shaped rifle bullet with a hollow base that expands when fired.

Pickets: Troops sent out in advance to warn of an enemy's approach.

Plantation: A large estate, often with resident workers, that produces income crops.

Raiders: Small groups of armed soldiers that detach from their main troops and force entry into a place, especially to steal valuables.

Reenactment: An event that attempts to accurately portray a past moment in history. People who participate in reenactments

are called *reenactors*.

Regiment: A military unit of ground troops. *Regimental* refers to something orderly and strict.

Review (as with soldiers): To conduct a military inspection.

Smokehouse: A place where meat or fish is preserved with smoke.

Sutlers: Army camp followers who provide items to the soldiers.

Sympathizer: To share the opinions and goals of a group, organization, or party.

Trench: A long, narrow ditch used for concealment and protection of soldiers during a battle.

Underground Railroad: A secret network of people who helped house and otherwise aid escaped slaves in their journey north to free states.

Veterans: People who have served in the armed forces.

Wardrobe: A cabinet built to hold clothes.

Whirligig: A toy that features parts that spin, often by means of a breeze.

Index

COBBLESTONE®
The CIVIL WAR Series

Few events in our nation's history have been as dramatic as those leading up to and during the Civil War. People held strong views on each side of the Mason-Dixon line, and the clash of North and South had far-reaching consequences for our country that are still being felt today.

Each 48-page book delivers the solidly researched content COBBLESTONE® is known for, written in an engaging manner that is sure to retain the attention of young readers. Perfect for report research or pursuing an emerging interest in the Civil War, these resources will complete your collection of materials on this important topic.

Each sturdy, hardcover volume includes:

- ■ Fair and balanced depictions of people and events
- ■ Well-researched text ■ Historical photographs
- ■ Glossary ■ Time line

$17⁹⁵ each

NATION AT WAR: SOLDIERS, SAINTS, AND SPIES	COB67900
YOUNG HEROES OF THE NORTH AND SOUTH	COB67901
ABRAHAM LINCOLN: DEFENDER OF THE UNION	COB67902
GETTYSBURG: BOLD BATTLE IN THE NORTH	COB67903
ANTIETAM: DAY OF COURAGE AND SACRIFICE	COB67904
ROBERT E. LEE: DUTY AND HONOR	COB67905
ULYSSES S. GRANT: CONFIDENT LEADER AND HERO	COB67906
STONEWALL JACKSON: SPIRIT OF THE SOUTH	COB67907
JEFFERSON DAVIS AND THE CONFEDERACY	COB67908
REBUILDING A NATION: PICKING UP THE PIECES	COB67909

Buy 3 books and get our Time Line Poster FREE!